When you touch
a loop in the thread,
it's time to stop
and use your head.
Inside loop one
is a question mark.
It tells you where
the riddles start.

Inside loop two
a letter gives
a clue to what
the answer is.
Write down the clues
in the order they come
and you'll learn who
this book is from.

clue

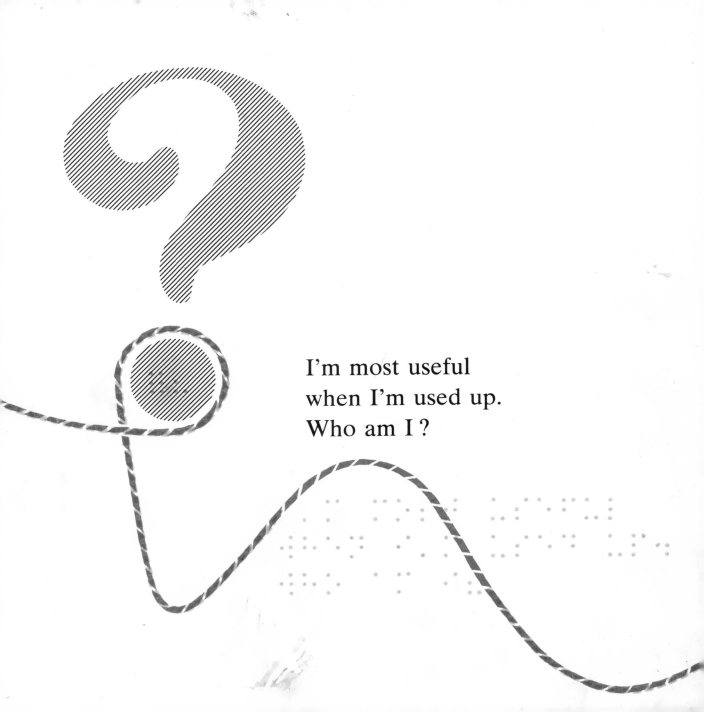

I'm most useful
when I'm used up.
Who am I ?

U

an umbrella

I have one eye
that cannot blink
or shed a tear.
Who am I ?

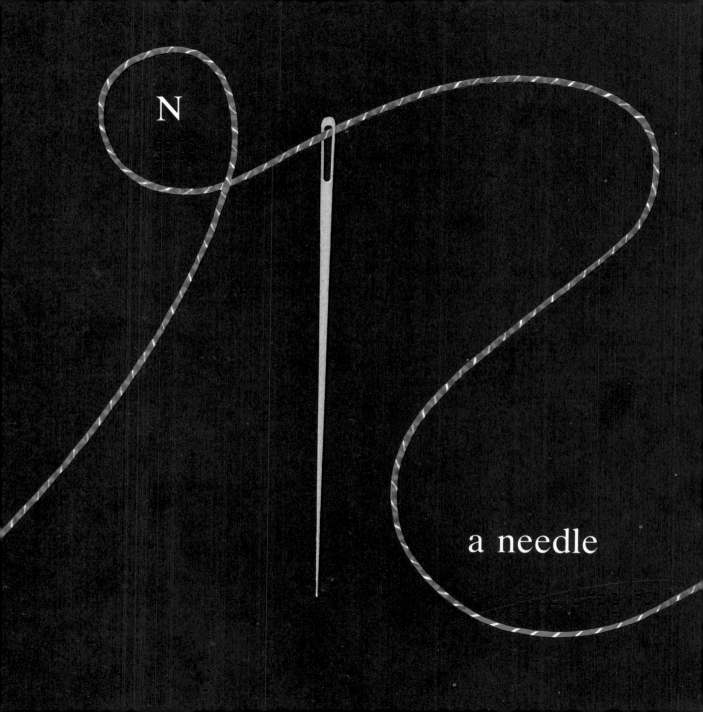

N

a needle

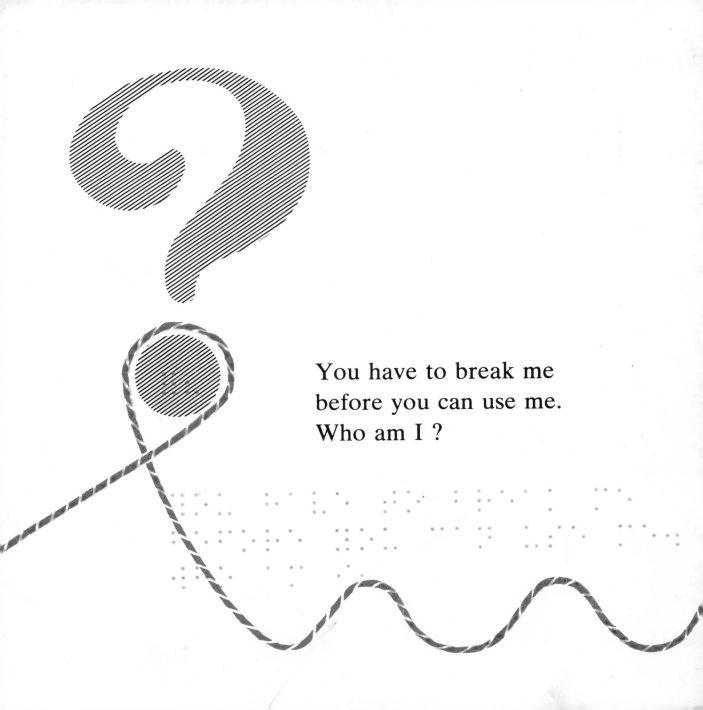

You have to break me
before you can use me.
Who am I ?

E

an egg

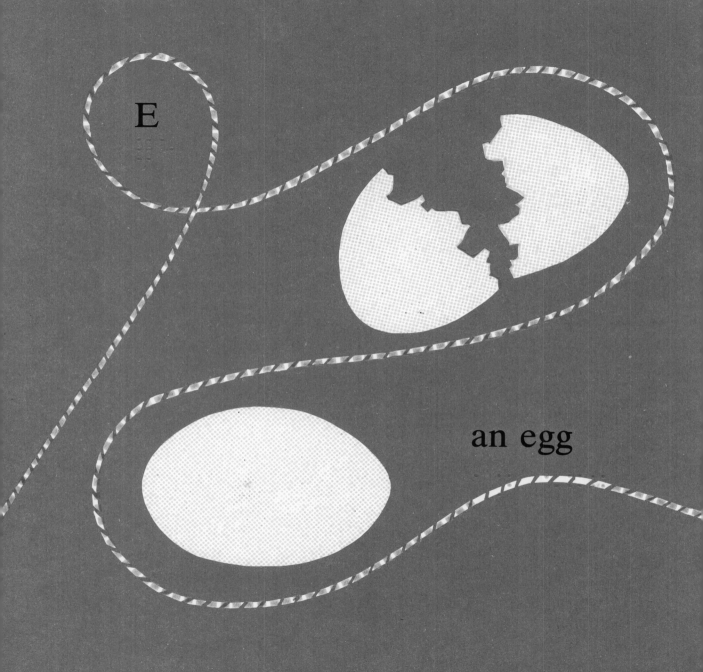

Open or closed
I am useless,
moving I cut
a nice figure.
Who am I ?

S

a scissors

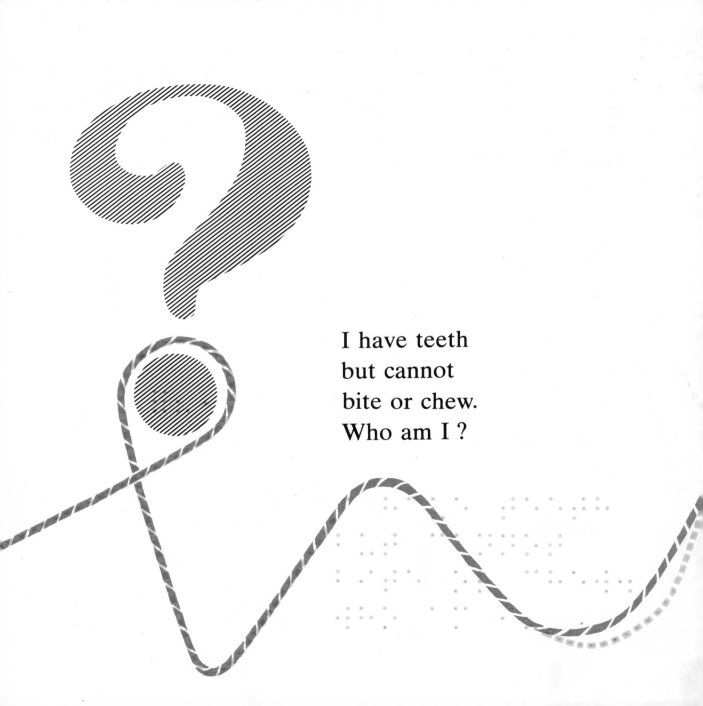

I have teeth
but cannot
bite or chew.
Who am I ?

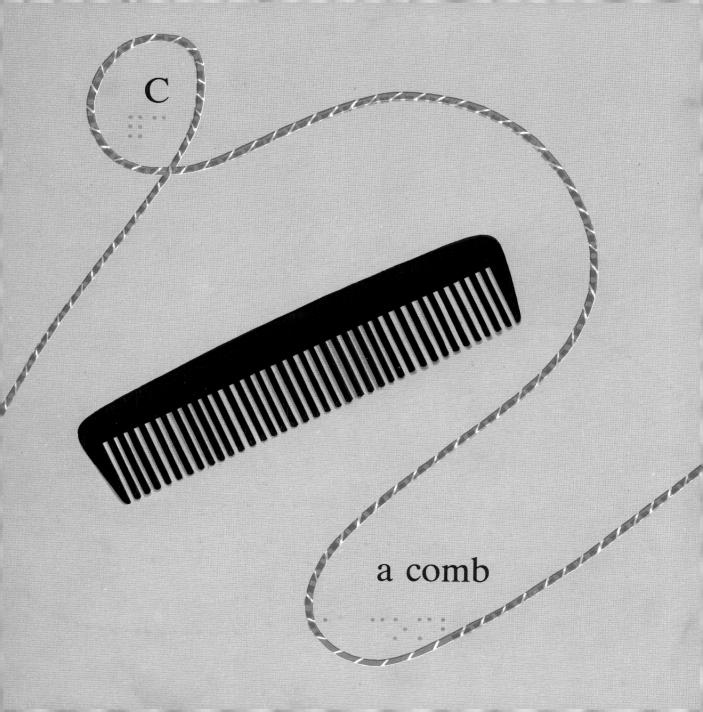

C

a comb

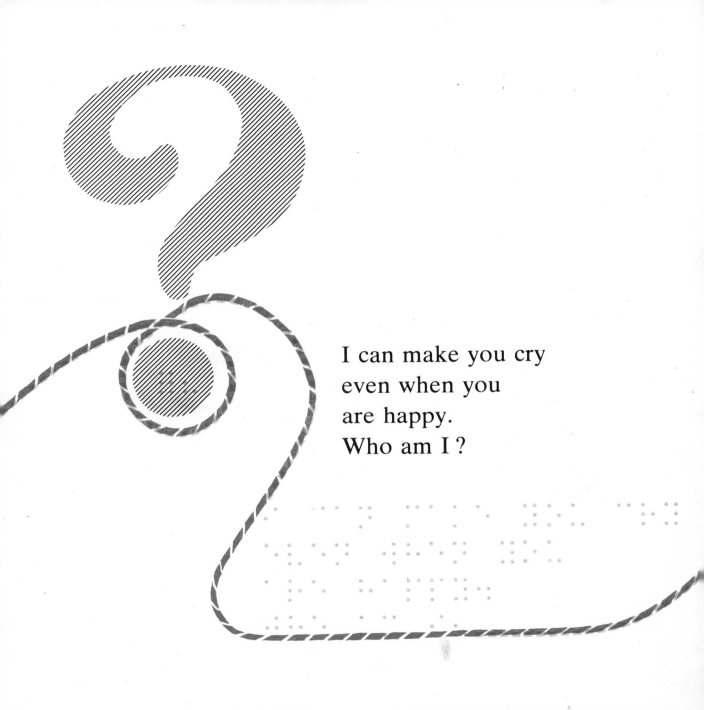

I can make you cry
even when you
are happy.
Who am I ?

O

an onion

Now read the clues,
all six of them.
The first is U,
the next is N.
Then comes an E,
an S, and a C.
The last is O –
who can it be ?

UNESCO

UNESCO made
this book for you
to give you something
fun to do
and tell you what
UNESCO is
and where and why
and who.

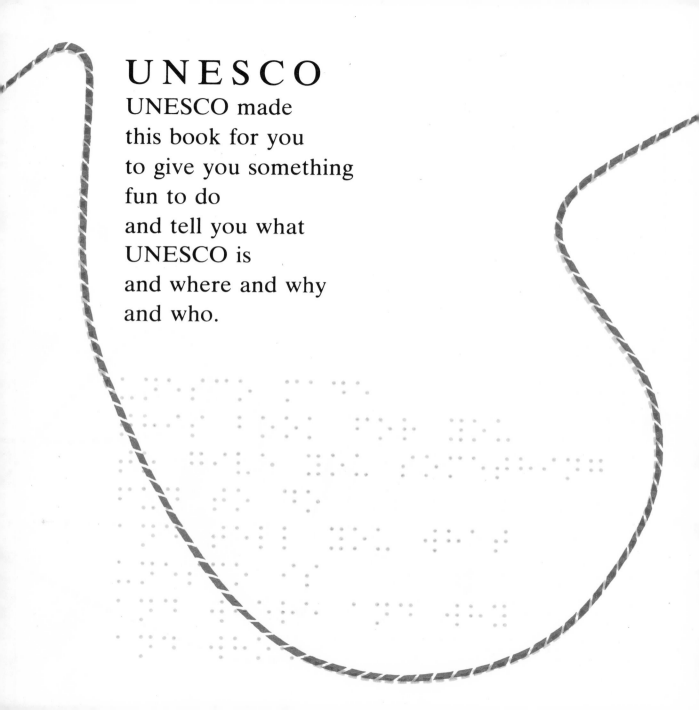

UNESCO is a place
where many people
from many lands
are working together
to try to solve
one of the greatest riddles
in the world.
Do you know what that riddle is ?

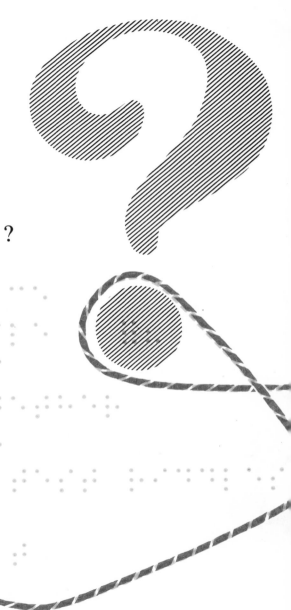

What can we do
to bring peace
to the world?
STOP FIGHTING
It's easier said than done,
but learning and playing together
will help us towards the goal.

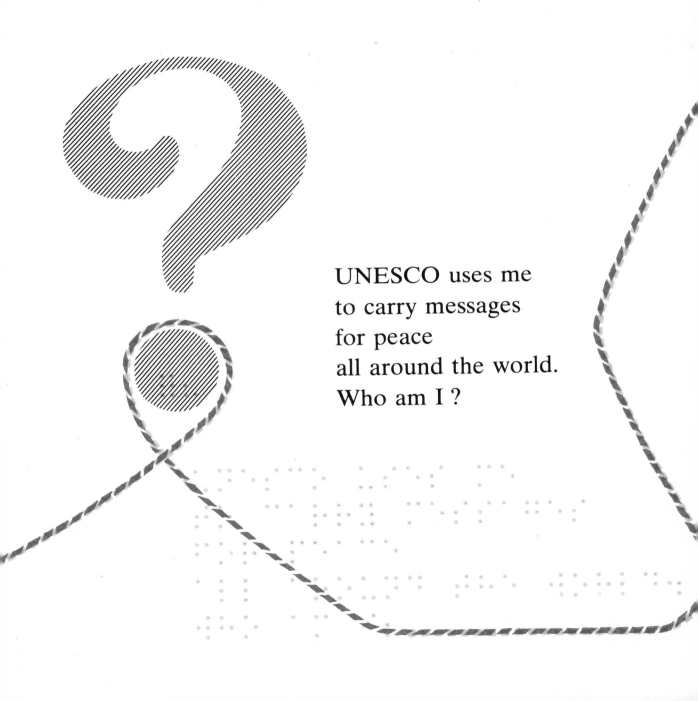

UNESCO uses me
to carry messages
for peace
all around the world.
Who am I ?

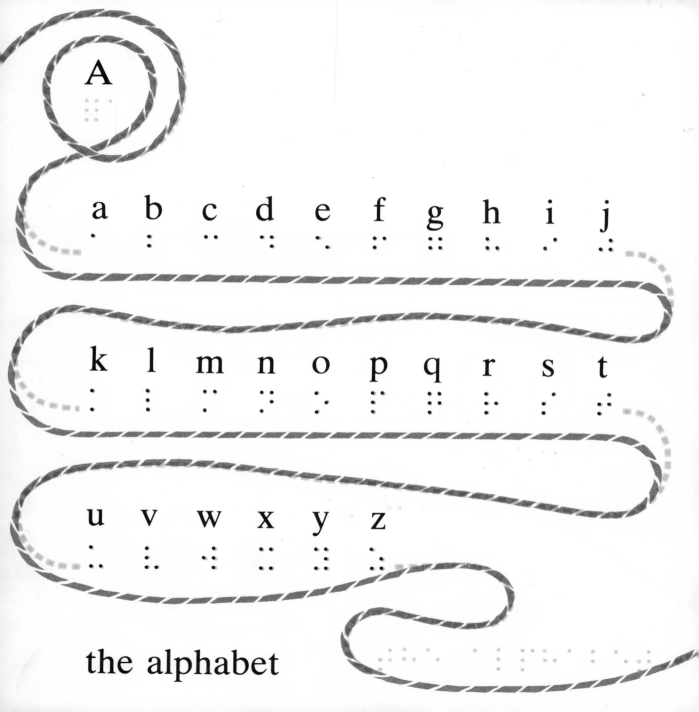

A

a b c d e f g h i j

k l m n o p q r s t

u v w x y z

the alphabet